To dr. Bo
from Leis

Horst van Cuyck

The Count and The Saint

Eustace and Ida of Boulogne

Horst van Cuyck

stichting kunstboek

By their fruit you will recognise them.

Do people pick grapes from thornbushes,
or figs from thistles? Likewise every good tree bears
good fruit, but a bad tree bears bad fruit.
A good tree cannot bear bad fruit,
and a bad tree cannot bear good fruit.
Every tree that does not bear good fruit
is cut down and thrown into the fire.
Thus, by their fruit you will recognise them.
(Matthew, 7:16-20).

King Edward the Confessor at table. 'Miscellaneous chronicles', 13th century. British Library, Cotton Claudius B.VI, fol. 87 v°.

Introduction

Eustace and Ida of Boulogne were a remarkable couple who lived in a remarkable time. He was one of the brave knights at the side of William the Conqueror in Hastings. He reigned over one of the most strategic counties in Western Europe, caught in a constant struggle for balance between war and bond, between power and alliance. She was the woman behind the man, well educated, intelligent and strong. She was his companion, the protector of the family and the family's reputation. She was a ruler who developed an impressive ecclesiastical network and consolidated comital power. She was to become the mother of the greatest crusader ever and was ultimately canonized.

The memory of Eustace and Ida has faded. Nine hundred years after Ida's death, it is time to bring them back to life.

Godfrey of Bouillon and his brother Baldwin I. William of Tyr, 'Historia', 13th century. Paris, Bibliothèque Nationale de France, Mss. Français 9081, fol. 65 v°.

The coastline in the neighbourhood of Wissant.

Eustace II, count of Boulogne

Eustace II was born in around 1015-1022. He was the oldest son of Eustace I, count of Boulogne, and Mathilda of Leuven, daughter of Lambert I, Count of Leuven, and Gerberga of Lower Lorraine. After the death of his father in 1047, Eustace II inherited the county of Boulogne, and his younger brother Lambert the county of Lens. When Lambert was killed in battle in 1054, Eustace II also inherited Lens.

As count of Boulogne, Eustace was a vassal of the King of France; as Count of Lens he was a vassal of the Count of Flanders, himself a vassal of the French King. But within his own territories Eustace was virtually a sovereign prince. The county of Boulogne was of great strategic and economic importance. The ships of Boulogne dominated the Channel. The port of Wissant handled most of the cross-Channel traffic and became the main port for importing English wool for the Flemish cloth trade.

'A man from the very highest birth'

The maternal ancestry of Count Eustace II was impressive. His mother, Mathilda of Louvain, was a granddaughter of Charles of Lorraine, the last lineal male descendant of Charlemagne. According to the contemporary *Genealogia Comitum Boloniensium* (Genealogy of the Counts of Boulogne), Eustace descended – via Charlemagne and the Merovingian Kings – from king Priam of Troy. Eustace's father also descended from Charlemagne through the marriage of Judith, the Emperor's great-granddaughter, with Baldwin I, Count of Flanders.

Eustace's dual Carolingian bloodline was the richest of any of his contemporaries and it gave him a lustre that was widely recognized. In the 11th century, the blood of Charlemagne was highly praised. The famous English chronicler Orderic Vitalis calls him *a man of the very highest birth, sprung from the stock of Charlemagne, most renowned king of the Franks.*

Through his father Eustace he also descended from Alfred the Great, through the marriage of the latter's daughter Elftrudis with Baldwin II of Flanders.

Eustace's brother Godfrey was Bishop of Paris. His other brother, Lambert, married the daughter of Robert I, duke of Normandy.

Statue of Charlemagne or Charles the Bald. Bronze, 9th century. Paris, Musée du Louvre. © RMN-Grand Palais (muse du Louvre) / Jean-Gilles Berizzi.

The count's nickname

Eustace's nickname in Old French was *Eustace als grenons* (*gernobadatus* in Latin), which means *Eustace with the long moustache or Eustace the whiskered.* The Count was apparently well known for his flowing moustaches and long whiskers. The earliest reference to his whiskers seems to be the *History of the Counts of Guines and the Lords of Ardres*, written by Lambert of Ardres between 1194 and 1198. On the Bayeux Tapestry, we see Eustace depicted with full moustache and whiskers. At the time of the Battle of Hastings, it was the fashion for the Normans and Frenchmen to wear their hair closely cropped at the back and have their faces clean-shaven. The English, on the contrary, typically wore moustaches. Count Eustace was an exceptional figure: a Frenchman with long whiskers and moustaches.

In around 633, an unmanned ship carrying just a statue of the Virgin Mary was sighted in the estuary at Boulogne. Some say that a swan pulled the boat. The statue glowed with white light and the townsfolk took it to the church for safekeeping. Soon miracles were reported at the site and the church with the Virgin of the Sea became a popular pilgrimage site. Pilgrims would come from England, France and Flanders. The town prospered: inns and hospices offered them food and lodging and they bought souvenirs such as small lead badges and candles.

The statue survived wars and religious troubles, but was finally completely destroyed during the French Revolution. Only a fragment of the hand remains.

Every year, on the last Monday of August, a modern replica of the statue is paraded around the city, a tradition that has been held since 1854. The statue wears a *soleil*, a resplendent headdress that is worn by the townswomen during the parade.

The Virgin of the Sea

Pilgrim badge of the Virgin of the Sea. Lead alloy, 14th century. British Museum, Dpt. Prehistory and Europe.

Our Lady of the Sea arrives in Boulogne. 'Manière de la foundation et augmentation de l'église Notre-Dame de Boulogne', 15th century. Bibliothèque nationale de France, Bibliothèque de l'Arsenal, Mss. 5126, fol. 6.

Old postcard with a photo of the Great Procession in Boulogne-sur-Mer. Private collection.

Goda

In 1035, Eustace married Goda or Godgifu, daughter of the English King Ethelred the Unready and his second wife Emma of Normandy. This marriage gave Eustace the opportunity to seal an alliance with the sons of his wife from her first marriage: Ralph, Count of Hereford, and Walter III, Count of Vexin and Amiens. When Goda's brother Edward the Confessor became King of England in 1042, Eustace became his loyal ally. But Goda was also related to the duke of Normandy, her mother being a daughter of Richard I of Normandy. Thus Eustace had strong ties to both England and Normandy. Through Goda, Eustace also acquired interest in a considerable amount of landed property in England.

It is generally accepted that Eustace and Goda had no children. The historian Frank Barlow is the only one to believe that the couple had a daughter who in turn had a son.

King Æthelred the Unready, seated, holding a sword.
'Chronicle of Abingdon', 13th century.
British Library, Cotton Claudius B. VI, fol. 87 v°.

Ida

In 1049, after Goda had died and left him without issue, Eustace married Ida, daughter of Godfrey the Bearded, duke of Upper Lorraine, and Doda. At that time, Godfrey openly rebelled against the German king Henry III. Pope Leo IX, who supported the German king, excommunicated Eustace II for incest (because Eustace and Ida were too closely related).

Baldwin I and a messenger.
'Cycle de la Croisade', 13th century.
Bibliothèque nationale de France,
Mss. Français 786, fol. 189 v°.

Eustace III, count of Boulogne.
Painting by Edouard Odier, 1844.
Versailles, Château de Versailles et de Trianon.

Godfrey of Bouillon.
Painting by Henri Leys, Oil on canvas, 19th century. Antwerp, Koninklijk Museum voor Schone Kunsten.

Baldwin of Boulogne.
Painting by Merry Joseph Blondel, 19th century. Versailles, Château de Versailles et de Trianon.

Eustace and Ida had four children:

Eustace III, who succeeded his father as Count of Boulogne and Lens in 1087.
He accompanied Robert II, Count of Flanders, on the First Crusade. In 1118, he was invited to succeed his brother Baldwin as King of Jerusalem, but when he was on his way to honour the invitation, he heard that Baudouin du Bourg had been chosen as king. He rested his claim and returned to Boulogne. Eustace III retired to the monastery of Cluny in 1125. He was married to Mary of Scotland, daughter of Malcolm III, King of Scotland, and his second wife (Saint) Margaret of Scotland. They had one daughter, Mathilda of Boulogne, who married Stephen of Blois, son of Stephen, Count of Blois, and his wife Adela of England. Stephen and Mathilda succeeded as Count and Countess of Boulogne in 1125. Stephen succeeded in 1135 as King of England. Mathilda was crowned Queen Consort of England at Westminster Abbey in 1136.
Godfrey of Bouillon, who inherited the County of Verdun, the allods of Stenay and Mouzay, and the castle of Bouillon with its dependencies. In 1087, he was installed Duke of Lower Lorraine.
He joined the First Crusade and became *princeps* (ruler) of Jerusalem in 1099.
Baldwin of Boulogne, Canon at Cambrai, Reims and Liège, who left the Church to become a knight. He was granted the county of Verdun in 1095, he was installed as Count of Edessa in 1098 and crowned King of Jerusalem in 1100.
Ida, who married firstly Herman van Malsen and secondly Cono, Count of Montaigu, son of Gozelo, Count of Montaigu and his wife Ermentrude of Grandpré. Ida was the matriarch of the Van Cuyck Family.

Eustace also had at least four illegitimate children by unknown mistresses.

Renowned spouses and progeny

Eustace's first wife was the daughter of King Eathelred the Unready and the sister of King Edward the Confessor. His second wife Ida of Boulogne also was a descendant of Charlemagne. Eustace's first father-in-law, Edward the Confessor, was canonized. Eustace's second wife, Ida of Boulogne, was also canonized. Eustace's sons became famous crusaders, of which Godfrey of Bouillon is the best known. Godfrey was the first ruler of Jerusalem and Defender of the Holy Sepulcher. Baldwin was the first King of Jerusalem. And Eustace III married Mary of Scotland, daughter of the Scottish King; their daughter became Queen of England as consort of Stephen of Blois.

Baldwin of Boulogne enters the city of Edessa. Painting by Joseph Nicolas Robert-Fleury, 19th century. Versailles, châteaux de Versailles et de Trianon. © RMN-Grand Palais (Château de Versailles) / Gérard Blot.

Godfrey of Bouillon accepts to become the defender of the Holy Sepulchre. Painting by Federico Madrazo y Kuntz, 19th century. Versailles, châteaux de Versailles et de Trianon. © RMN-Grand Palais (Château de Versailles) / Gérard Blot.

Saint Ida says goodbye to her sons. 'Enfance Godefroi', 13th century. Bibliothèque nationale de France, Mss. Français 786, fol. 165 v°.

Godfrey of Bouillon and Baldwin of Boulogne are crossing the Bosphorus. Baldwin is accompanied by his wife and children. Painting by Emile Signol, 19th century. Versailles, châteaux de Versailles et de Trianon. © RMN-Grand Palais (Château de Versailles) / Gérard Blot.

King Harold of England. 'Chroniques d'Angleterre', 15th century. Bibliothèque nationale de France, Mss. Français 75, fol. 207 v°.

Ally of England

In August or September 1051, Eustace travelled to England to discuss matters with king Edward the Confessor. It is likely that Eustace conferred with Edward about the latter's succession. The king's marriage to Edith of Wessex had remained childless and he was making preparations to appoint a successor. Eustace probably advocated the claims of his stepsons (the sons of his wife and Edward's sister Goda and her first husband Drogo of Mantes, Count of the Véxin). Perhaps he himself was a candidate for the English kingship?

On the count's return, an armed conflict broke out between Eustace's party and the citizens of Dover. As different sources contradict each other, the circumstances of this incident are not clear. In any case, Godwin of Wessex, the most powerful earl of England (and father-in-law of Edward the Confessor), refused to punish the town of Dover and Eustace prepared himself for battle against Godwin and his supporters. King Edward, however, sought a peaceful solution through a trial of Godwin and his sons, the affair ultimately resulting in the banishment of Godwin and his family. Eustace maintained friendly relations with King Edward, even if he was an adversary of Earl Godwin and his sons.

Pope Urban II on his way to Clermont and the same preaching at the Council. William of Tyr, 'Historia', 14th century. Paris, Bibliothèque Nationale de France, Mss. Français 22495, fol. 15.

In March 1095, the Byzantine emperor Alexios I Komnenos sent envoys to Pope Urban II to ask for aid against the Turks. Urban responded favourably and started recruiting men for the expedition. At the Council of Clermont, a few months later, he gave an impassioned sermon to a large audience of French nobles and clergy. It is said that the enthusiastic crowd responded with cries of *Deus vult*! (God wills it!). Adhemar of Le Puy was the first to take the cross. Godfrey of Bouillon, son of Eustace II and Ida, took out loans on most of his lands, or sold them. With this money he gathered thousands of knights to fight in the Holy Land. His older brother, Eustace, and his younger brother, Baldwin, joined him in his effort.

The crusaders' armies left Europe in August 1096. They gathered outside the walls of Constantinople and continued their journey in 1097, to finally reach Jerusalem on 7 June 1099. The major attack on the city took place on 14 and 15 July 1099. Godfrey and some of his knights were the first to get over the walls and enter the city.

Godfrey of Bouillon and the First Crusade

The kingdom of Jerusalem was established and Godfrey of Bouillon became its leader, but refused to be crowned king in the city where Christ had died. The sources are not clear about his exact title: 'Defender of the Holy Sepulcher', 'Duke' or 'Princeps'. The title 'King of Jerusalem' was borne by his brother and successor Baldwin.
Godfrey had to defend the new Kingdom of Jerusalem against the Fatimids of Egypt and his campaigns of the following months enabled him to force other cities like Caesarea and Jaffa to become tributaries.

Godfrey died on 18 July 1100. The cause of his death is not clear. Some say that he was killed by an arrow while besieging the city of Acre, others say that he fell ill, still others claim that he was poisoned. He was buried in the church of the Holy Sepulcher.
According to William of Tyre, the later 12th-century chronicler of the Kingdom of Jerusalem, Godfrey was *tall of stature, not extremely so, but still taller than the average man. He was strong beyond compare, with solidly built limbs and a stalwart chest. His features were pleasing, his beard and hair of medium blond.*
Being the first ruler of Jerusalem, Godfrey became a legend. He was believed to have possessed immense physical strength and became a hero in the *chansons de geste* of the Crusaders Cycle. The *trouvères* provided him with a mythical origin, making him a descendant of the legendary Swan Knight.

Godfrey of Bouillon refuses to be crowned King of Jerusalem. William of Tyr, 'Historia', 13th century. Paris, Bibliothèque Nationale de France, Mss. Français 9081, fol. 88 v^{c}.

Death of Godrey of Bouillon and coronation of his brother and successor Baldwin. William of Tyr, 'Historia', 13th century. Paris, Bibliothèque Nationale de France, Mss. Français 2623, fol. 79.

Godfrey of Bouillon puts his sword on Christ's grave. Drawing by Nicaise De Keyser, 19th century. Antwerp, Koninklijk Museum voor Schone Kunsten.

The Harold stone at Battle Abbey.

Reconstruction drawing of
the interior of the abbey church in
the 12th century by Peter Urmston.

EUSTACE AND THE BATTLE OF HASTINGS

Eustace played a significant role at the Battle of Hastings in 1066, as is clear from the wealth attributed to him in Domesday Book. Count Eustace II was certainly present at the Battle of Hastings. He was a powerful and illustrious ally of William the Conqueror, but accounts of his role in the battle differ greatly.

In the *Gesta Guillelmi* (The deeds of William) of William of Poitiers (written between 1071 and 1077), Eustace is depicted as a coward who advises Duke William to retreat before suffering a blow in the back and being carried off the battlefield more dead than alive. This Norman account of the battle stressed the importance of William's role at Hastings and diminished the contribution of Eustace, who had fallen into disgrace since his attempt to attack Dover in 1067.

Harold is being shot in the eye by an arrow and afterwards slain to death. Bayeux Tapestry, 11th century. Bayeux, Musée de la Tapisserie.

The *Carmen de Hastingae Proelio*, written by Bishop Guy of Amiens in as early as 1068, provides us with a very different and probably more accurate account of Eustace's role. Duke William was unhorsed and Eustace valiantly gave up his own warhorse for William's use. Eustace took another horse and continued to fight at William's side. *By their two swords they clear the battlefield of English troops.* Eustace continued to fight to the end and led William to victory.

The Bayeux Tapestry confirms the important role Eustace played in the Battle of Hastings. Without Eustace and his knights, the battle might have been lost for William. The climax of the battle was, of course, the death of Harold. On the Tapestry we can see that Harold is struck in the eye by an arrow; he is slain in the next scene by a knight with a sword.

According to the *Carmen de Hastingae Proelio*, Harold was attacked by William, Eustace of Boulogne, Hugh of Ponthieu, and Giffard: *these four bore arms for the destruction of the king.* Each of these four delivers a mortal blow to Harold: *The first of the four [Duke William of Normandy], piercing the king's shield and chest with his lance, drenched the ground with a gushing stream of blood. The second [Count Eustace of Boulogne] with his sword*

After the Battle of Hastings, the victorious Normans leave their tents, while relatives of the English soldiers seek their dead, and four monks carry Harold's body to Waltham Abbey for burial 'Chronique de Normandie', 15th century. British Library, Yates Thompson 33, fol. 167.

cut off his head below the protection of his helm. The third [Hugh of Ponthieu] liquefied his entrails with his spear. And the fourth [Robert Gilfard] cut off his thigh and carried it some distance away.

When we look at the Tapestry, it seems at first as if the artisan leaves us guessing about the identity of the knight who cuts Harold to the ground. But upon closer inspection, we can see that the helmet of the knight points horizontally at the letters TUS:EST (separated out of the words INTERFECTUS EST). There was no reason for the artist to separate these letters from the rest of the words. So then, why did he do so? What is the hidden message? If we reverse the two triplets TUS:EST, we get EST:TUS, which could be an abbreviation for EUSTATIUS. The wing of the bird in the upper border and the sword of the man in the next scene both point at the letters.

Eustace II and the Bayeux Tapestry

William is at a banquet held in his honour, flanked by his barons and Bishop Odo. The council sits immediately afterwards.
Bayeux Tapestry, 11th century.
Bayeux, Musée de la Tapisserie.

The Bayeux Tapestry is a beautifully embroidered piece of linen of about 70 meters long and 50 centimetres high, depicting the story of Harold Godwinson and William the Bastard, duke of Normandy, and the succession of the English throne in 1066. From the 18th century onwards, the Tapestry was known as *La Tapisserie de la Reine Mathilde* (The Tapestry of Queen Mathilda). People believed that the embroidery was the work of Queen Mathilda, William the Conqueror's wife: while her husband was away to conquer England, Mathilda filled her long and lonely evenings embroidering the Tapestry.

Scholars have long since abandoned the belief that the Tapestry was embroidered or even commissioned by Queen Mathilda, and for a long time it was widely accepted that Bishop Odo of Bayeux, William the Conqueror's half-brother, was the most likely patron of the work. But the case for Odo is conjectural and in 1999 Andrew Bridgeford argued that Eustace II was the Tapestry's patron.
Odo of Bayeux certainly is a good candidate. The Tapestry gives him a prominent place in the story, greater than other contemporary sources. According to the Tapestry, Harold took his oath

Duke William, to prove that he is not dead, lifts up his helmet to show himself to the troops. His ally, count Eustace II of Boulogne, is pointing at him.
Bayeux Tapestry, 11th century.
Bayeux, Musée de la Tapisserie.

in favour of William at Odo's cathedral city of Bayeux. Two minor characters named in the Tapestry, Wadard and Vital, can be identified as tenants of Odo in post-Conquest Kent. Moreover, the Tapestry has long been connected with the Cathedral of Bayeux. Since the Tapestry shows various characteristics of English design and manufacture, it could have been made in Kent, Odo's power base in England after the Conquest, perhaps at St. Augustine's in Canterbury.

It is widely accepted that the Tapestry does not represent the most authentic, most aggressive point of view of the events. The work is sympathetic to the memory of Harold, who is not at all depicted as the villain and cruel murderer the chronicler William of Poitiers makes him out to be. In the written sources, Odo is described as an extremely ambitious person whose attitude toward the defeated English was at the best one of disdain and at worst one of outright cruelty. The contradiction between the Tapestry's version of events and Odo's attitude towards the English creates some doubt as to the bishop's patronage of the embroidery.

William I, the Conqueror, holding a sword and scepter.
Sir Thomas Holme's Book of Arms, 15th century. British Library, Harley 4205, fol. 1. © The British Library Board.

Eustace II seems the more likely candidate as patron of the Tapestry. The Count was one of William's most powerful and prestigious non-Norman allies at Hastings and he takes a prominent place in the Tapestry. At a crucial moment in the battle, he turns around to point to Duke William as the latter raises his nosepiece to dispel rumours of his death. Since we know that Eustace rebelled against the Normans in 1067 by attacking Dover castle, it is odd that Eustace should take such a prominent place in the Tapestry. In fact it is odd that he is depicted at all if indeed the Tapestry was commissioned by the Bishop of Bayeux. But knowing that Dover castle in fact belonged to Odo who is also given a prominent place in the Tapestry, we may assume that Eustace was the Tapestry's patron and that it was intended as a gift from Eustace to Odo, and as such formed part of the process of their reconciliation after the Dover attack. In any case, the choice of Odo and Eustace as the only named battle companions of the Conqueror attests to the fact that the relation between them was a fundamental reason for the creation of the Tapestry. Susan Brown believes that the sequential arrangement of the chosen highlights of the Battle of Hastings in the Bayeux Tapestry was carefully orchestrated so as to present the ultimate French victory as a direct result of an action that originated in the alliance between Odo of Bayeux, William the Conqueror and Eustace II of Boulogne.

There are other elements underlying the importance of Eustace in the Tapestry. His name is captioned as a single word in the upper border. Eustace's banner is the largest and most elaborate one in the whole Tapestry. And the archer depicted directly below Eustace is the only coloured one. All these elements draw the eye to the Count of Boulogne.

The banner

On the Bayeux Tapestry, Eustace is holding a banner in his hands. It is the largest banner on the Tapestry and several scholars believe this to be the famous papal banner. According to William of Poitiers, Pope Alexander II blessed William's expedition and sent a papal banner that was borne at Hastings together with a ring containing a hair of Saint Peter. According to Orderic Vitalis, however, this banner was borne by Turstin, the son of Rollo.

The banner could be an additional element to help identify the figure holding it. The device on the banner – a cross shape cantoned by four disks – can be found on Eustace's coinage, but also on a large variety of early medieval coinage throughout Europe. More convincing is the similarity between the device on the banner and the symbol used to identify Saint Eustachius in medieval times. Saint Eustachius was converted to Christianity after receiving a vision: while he was hunting a stag, he saw a cross between the stag's antlers. The drawing on the banner in the Tapestry can be seen as a stylized representation of the cross in the stag's antlers. The disks may also refer to the coat of arms of the County of Boulogne.

Vision of Saint Eustace.
Vincent de Beauvais,
'Miroir d'Histoire', 14th century
Bibliothèque nationale de France,
Bibliothèque de l'Arsenal,
Mss. 5080, fol. 124 v°.

Edward the Confessor sends Harold Godwinson to Normandy to inform Duke William that he is to succeed him on the English throne.
Bayeux Tapestry, 11th century.
Bayeux, Musée de la Tapisserie.

1066

The English king Edward the Confessor died childless on 4 or 5 January 1066. He was buried in Westminster abbey on 6 January and Harold Godwinson was crowned King of England that same day. This Harold was not only the former king's brother-in-law, but also the most powerful earl in the kingdom. It is possible that on his deathbed, Edward the Confessor entrusted the kingdom to Harold, but there certainly were other candidates for the throne.
Edgar the Ætheling, grandson of Edward the Confessor's half-brother Edmund Ironside, was definitely a favorite of the king for a time. Yet he had little support, and was unable to defend his claim through military action.
Harald Hardrada, king of Norway, also claimed the English throne and invaded the country with the support of Tostig Godwinson, Harold Godwinson's brother. Both were defeated and killed in the Battle of Stamford Bridge on 25 September 1066. The third claimant to the throne was William the Bastard, duke of Normandy. He was related to Edward the Confessor through the latter's mother Emma of Normandy. The Norman claimed that Edward had sent Harold Godwinson to Normandy in about 1064 to confirm the promise of the succession to him. As soon as de duke heard of Harold's coronation, he assembled a fleet and invaded England. William defeated and killed Harold in the Battle of Hastings on 14 October 1066. After the battle, he marched to London and was crowned at Westminster Abbey on Christmas Day. His consort Mathilda of Flanders was crowned queen on 11 May 1068.

Duke William of Normandy, the Conqueror, stabs King Harold of England at the Battle of Hastings as they fight on horseback, whilst men clear up after the battle. Miscellaneous chronicles', 13th century. British Library, Cotton Claudius B.VI, fol. 87 v°.

The Battle of Stamford Bridge. Mattew Paris, 'The Life of Edward the Confessor', 13th century. Cambridge, University Library, MS. Ee.3.59, fol. 32 v°. Reproduced by kind permission of the Syndics of Cambridge University Library.

The Aftermath of 1066

Eustace returned to the Continent in 1067, and led an attack on Dover that same year. More specifically, he attacked Dover castle, which William had entrusted to his half-brother Odo, Bishop of Bayeux. It was a well-planned attack, timed to coincide with the absence of Odo and his knights. Although Eustace had the support of a large contingent from the nearby regions, the knights were scattered. A kinsman of Eustace was captured, but Eustace himself managed to escape and returned to Boulogne. In the end the attempt to seize Dover turned out to be a disaster: a close kinsman of Eustace was taken prisoner, the Count himself was condemned and his lands in England were forfeited.

A few years later, Eustace reached reconciliation with William the Conqueror and was granted a large English lordship. After William's father-in-law, Count Baldwin V of Flanders, died in 1067, he tried to find a strong ally in the region. In 1071, Eustace and William both supported Arnulf III, the minor Count of Flanders, and his mother and guardian Richilde of Hainault, against the usurper Robert the Frisian. When the latter allied himself with Philip I of France, William depended on Eustace to protect the northern border of his duchy. Moreover, it was very convenient for William to be able to use the short sea crossing from Wissant to Dover. Also, Eustace's brother Godfrey, Bishop of Paris and chancellor to the French King, would have been an interesting contact for William. As for Eustace, William was an important ally in his attempt to maintain and enhance his independence from Flanders. The reconciliation certainly took place before 1086: in that year Eustace was the tenth richest landholder recorded in Domesday Book.

In the early 1080s, a genealogy of the comital family of Boulogne was produced which stressed Eustace's Carolingian descent through his mother, Mathilda, and his marriage to Ida of Lorraine, and also reflected the prestige the family had gained through Eustace's military prowess.
Eustace died in 1087.

The pious spouse

Eustace's second wife, Ida of Boulogne, was born in Bouillon in around 1040. She was the daughter of Godfrey II the Bearded, duke of Upper Lorraine. She is called Ida of Boulogne, Ida of Verdun or Ida of Lorraine.
During her childhood, Ida was sent to the abbey of Bilzen (in Belgium), where she received her education. She was also under the supervision of her paternal uncle, cardinal Frederic of Lorraine, archdeacon of Liège and future pope Etienne IX. Ida's mother, Doda, and her grandfather Gozelon, were buried in the monastery of Bilzen.

Painting representing Saint Ida and her three sons. Church of Le Wast.

According to her *Vita*, Ida was beautiful, tall and blond. She was a pious woman who led a virtuous Christian life. After her husband's death, she devoted her life to the Church. She made many donations to religious houses and founded and restored several monasteries. She was renowned for her donations to the poor. She did not take the habit of a Benedictine nun, as some have argued, but through the Abbot Hugh of Cluny, she obtained spiritual aggregation with the monastery of Cluny. She corresponded with Saint Anselm of Canterbury and maintained contact with the Spanish Bishop Osmond of Astorga.
She died on 13 April 1113.

Tomb of Hugues of Cluny (bottom). Drawing by Alexandre Lenoir, 19th century. Paris, Musée du Louvre.

Statue of Saint Ida in the church of Le Wast.

Biography of a saint

Statue of Saint Ida in the church of Le Wast.

Mathilda of Boulogne, daughter of Eustace III and wife of Stephen of Blois, urged the Church authorities to canonize her grandmother Ida of Boulogne. Mathilda's other grandmother, Margaret of Scotland, had already been canonized by that time. The canonization of Ida was part of the campaign to make Stephen King of England. The monks of the Priory of Le Wast, the guardians of Ida's grave, were asked to write her biography.

After the prologue, the biography can be divided into three parts: (1) her childhood, marriage and motherhood; (2) her life as a widow; (3) miracles and other events that took place at her grave. It is interesting to see how her biographer is in fact reluctant toward the idea of a female married saint. How can a married woman, not a virgin, become a saint? The text places great emphasis on the need for wives to submit to their husbands and on the reproductive function of the female body. *Virginity is good, but chastity after childbirth is great.* Ida was a link in a genealogical chain. She married Count Eustace, a hero, *of most noble race and of the blood of Charlemagne.*

Ida was a good Christian wife, pious, obedient and discreet in the management of her home. But most important of all, she was chaste. She conceived children *according to the apostolic precept*, which means *by using her husband as though she had no husband,* eschewing pleasure. Her many merits incude her

Stain glass window representing Saint Ida. Samer, Église paroissiale Saint-Martin, actuellement chapelle Notre-Dame, place du Maréchal-Foch.

giving birth to three sons, among them the King of Jerusalem. According to her biographer, Ida insisted on breast-feeding her children herself, because she feared that her children might otherwise be exposed to bad influences. We find the same story in the *Cycle de la Croisade*.

As a saint, she obviously performed miracles. One day, a little girl who was unable to speak took refuge under her cloak. After that, the child began to speak. Her first word was 'mother'. One day, when Ida was in England, she gave alms to a cripple. As soon as he accepted the gift, he was cured. The sick came to her from far and wide and she cured them through prayers and lying of hands.

After her death, the number of miracles increased. Mathilda, Ida's granddaughter and wife of Stephen of Blois, was one of the many who were cured.

A few years after her death, Ida's grave was opened up in the presence of many who had gathered from miles around. Her body appeared to be completely intact, as were her clothes. A pleasant smell arose from the grave: a sign of saintliness.

Ida of Boulogne was canonized, especially thanks to the efforts of her granddaughter Mathilda. King Louis XI of France named her patron saint of the town and county of Boulogne in April 1478.

Statue of Saint Ida in the Basilica of Boulogne-sur-Mer.

The Great Domesday Book in five volumes, 11th century. London, The National Archives of the UK, E31-1 and E31-2.

Fragment of Domesday Book, 11th century. London, The National Archives of the UK, E31-2, fol. 51.

In the Anglo-Saxon Chronicle we read: *While spending the Christmas time of 1085 in Gloucester, William had deep speech with his counsellors and sent men all over England to each shire to find out what or how much each landholder had in land and livestock, and what it was worth.* The main purpose of the survey was to determine who held what and what taxes had been liable under Edward the Confessor.

After the Norman conquest of England and the confiscation of a lot of landed property, it was important to have an inventory of the names of the new holders of lands and the assessments on which their tax was to be paid. It became possible for William to see the extent of a given baron's possessions and made clear in how far he had engaged under-tenants, and whom those under-tenants were.

A survey approaching the scope and extent of the Domesday Book was not attempted until the Return of Owners of Land (1873) which presented the first subsequent complete picture of the distribution of landed property in the British Isles and is in this way sometimes referred to as the 'Modern Domesday'.

Domesday book

IN NOVA FORESTA & CIRCA EA. IN RODBRIGE HD.

Rex habuit 7 ht' unā hidā in Achelie. 7 de firma
insulæ Wit'. Cheping tenuit in paragio. Tc se defd p una
hida. m p nichilo. Tra. ē. iii. car.
T.R.E. 7 post ualuit. l. sol. Modo. ē in foresta. Ibi erā rex misit.

Walchelin eps habuit in Falelie unā hid 7 iii. v træ.
7 p tanto geldau. Modo p nichilo. Tra. ē. xii. car.
T.R.E. 7 post ualuit. l. sol. modo. ē in foresta. IN BOVRE HD.

Isd eps habuit Truhā in dnio 7 fuit in monasterio. ē. ii.
hid 7 dim se defdb. Tra. ē. iiii. car.
T.R.E. 7 post. ualb. lx. sol. modo. ē in foresta.

Isd eps habuit Selive in dnio 7 fuit sep in monasterio.
p. iii. hid se defd. Tra. ē. viii. car.
T.R.E. 7 post. ualb. x. lib. Modo. ē in foresta. excepto pto
qd adhuc tenet qui ōm tenuit. viii. ac sunt pti.

Rogerius comes habuit Lesteorde. Duo alodiarii
tenuer in paragio. 7 defdb sh tra p una hida.
T.R.E. 7 post. ualb. xl. sol. Modo. ē in foresta excepta. iiii.
parte uni v. quā ten qdā ho de comite. 7 ibi ht. iii. bord.

Ipse com ten in Svei. una hid 7 Fulcoin de eo. Val. iii. sol.
Alured tenuit in paragio. Tc se defd p una hida. m p. iii. v
7 iiii. v. ē in foresta. Tra. ē. i. car in dnio. Ibi. iiii. bord hnt dimid
car. 7 una ac pti. T.R.E. 7 post. 7 modo. ualt. x. sol. Qd rex ht. ii. sol.

Ipse com ht in Svei una hid 7 Nigel de eo. Durand tenuit in
paragio. Tc se defd p una hida. m p una. v. aliæ sunt in foresta.
Ibi. ii. uitti hnt. i. car. 7 dim ac pti.
Valuit. xx. sol. modo. v. sol. Qd rex ht. xv. sol.

Ipse com ht in Bedeslei unā hid 7 Durand de eo. Suarang
tenuit in paragio. Tc se defd p una hida. Modo p una v. aliæ
sunt in foresta. Tra. ē. i. car. Ibi. i. uitts 7 iii. bord hnt. i. car.

Ipse com ht in Oselei unā hid. 7 Nigell de eo. Val. iii. sol.
Saulf tenuit in paragio. Tc se defd p una hida. modo. ē
in foresta excepta una ac pti. q ten Nigell. Valb. xl. sol.

Ipse com ten unā hid in Oselei 7 Fulcuinus de eo. Goduin
tenuit in paragio. Tc se defd p una hida. m est in foresta.
excepto. ii. acris pti. Tra fuit. ii. car. 7 ualb. xx. sol.

Ipse com habuit ... ōm Truchā 7 Witts de eo. Colgrin
7 Eduui tenuer in paragio. 7 defdb se p. ii. hid 7 dimid.
Modo tot in foresta. Tra fuit. iiii. car. Valb. lx. sol.

Ipse com ten in Wolnetune dimid hida. 7 Fulcuin de eo. Alnod
tenuit in paragio. Tc p dim hida. m p una v. Tra. ē. i. car. 7 ibi
ē in dnio. cu uno bord. 7 uno seruo. T.R.E. ualb. xv. sol. 7 post 7 m.
x. sol. Silua. ē in foresta. 7 ual. iii. sol.

Ipse com ten. i. hid in Lentune. 7 Fulcuin de eo. Leuing tenuit
in paragio. Tc p una hida. m p dim. qa silua. ē in foresta. Tra. ē
ii. car. Ibi un uitts. ii. serui. iii. bord hnt. i. car. 7 iii. ac pti.
T.R.E. ualb. xx. sol. 7 post 7 m. xv. sol.

Ipse com ht in Hentune dim hid. 7 Fulcuin de eo. Vluui tenuit
in paragio. Tc p dim hida. m p una v 7 dim. qa alia. ē in foresta.
Tra. ē. i. car. 7 ibi. ē cu. iii. uittis. 7 una ac pti 7 dim. Val 7 ualuit
xv. sol. Qd rex ht. iii. solid.

Ipse com ht in Esselie. v. uirg 7 dim. 7 Nigell de eo. Saolf
tenuit in paragio. Tc se defd p. v. uirg 7 dim. m p. iii. v 7 dim.
Vna v ē in foresta. Tra. ē. iii. car. 7 ibi. ē in dnio. 7 ii. uitti 7 x.
bord cu. ii. car. 7 v. ac pti 7 dim. Valuit. l. sol. modo. xx. sol.
Qd rex ht. vi. sol.

Ipse com ht in Beraminetune. vii. uirg. 7 Durand de eo.
Aluric tenuit de rege. E. Tc p vii. uirg. m p. v. uirg.
qa aliæ sunt in foresta. Tra. ē. iii. car. In dnio. ē una. 7 iii. uitti
7 iii. bord hnt. i. car. Ibi. ii. serui. vi. sol.
T.R.E. ualb. xl. sol. 7 post. xxx. sol. Modo. xx. sol. Qd rex ht.

Ipse com ht. i. hid in Burminetune. 7 Durand de eo.
Wluuard tenuit in paragio. Tc p una hida. modo p dim.
alia. ē in foresta. Tra. ē. i. car. 7 ibi. ē in dnio. cu. i. bord.
7 dim ac pti. Valuit. xx. sol. modo. x. sol. Qd rex ht. vi. sol.

Ipse com ht in Hentune. i. hida. 7 Nigell de eo. Edric
tenuit in paragio. Tc p una hida. m p. iii. uirg. una. ē in
foresta. Tra. ē. iii. car. Ibi. vi. uitti hnt. ii. car. 7 vi. ac pti.
Val 7 ualuit. xv. solid. Qd rex ht. iii. sol.

Ipse com ht in Bichelei. unā hid. 7 Nigell de eo. Ho
lengar tenuit in paragio. Tc p una hida. m p. iii. uirg.
una v. ē in foresta. Tra. ē. iiii. car. Ibi. iii. uitti hnt. ii. car.
7 iiii. ac pti. Valuit. xx. sol. modo. xv. sol. Qd rex ht. v. sol.

Ipse com ten in Fernehelle tciā parte uni hide.
7 Nigell ten de com. Godric tenuit in paragio. Tc se defd
p. iii. uirg. modo p una v. aliæ sunt in foresta. Tra. ē. i. car.
7 ibi. ē cu uno uitto. Valuit. xiii. sol. modo. x. sol. Qd rex

II. Witts de ow ten un ōm In Rodedic HD. Ten. iii. sol.
7 Bernard de eo. Coolf tenuit de rege. E. Tc se defd
p. ii. hid. m p. v. uirg. Tra. ē. iii. car. Ibi. iii. uitti 7 ii.
bord hnt. ii. car. 7 vi. ac pti. T.R.E. 7 post. ualt. xl. sol.
Modo. xxx. sol. Rex ht. i. uirg cu silua. ualt. v. sol.

V. Radulf de mortemer ten Herdel. 7 Odelard de eo.
Iustan tenuit de rege. E. Tc p v. hid. m p. iiii. hid.
qnta. ē in foresta. Tra. ē. v. car. Ibi. vi. uitti 7 x. bord
hnt. iii. car. Ibi moliñ 7 vi. saline de. xv. denar.
T.R.E. ualb. viii. lib. 7 post. c. sol. 7 m similit. Silua
ten rex in foresta. ubi maneb. vi. hoes. Valet. lx. sol.

VI. Hugo de port ten in Pisteslei unā v
7 dim. 7 Hugo de eo. Algar tenuit in paragio. Tc se defd
p una v 7 dim. Modo p nichilo qa tota. ē in foresta.
excepta. i. ac pti 7 dim. Tra fuit. i. car. Valuit. x. sol.

Isd Hugo ten unā hidā in Truhā. 7 Hugo de eo.
Wislac tenuit in paragio. Tc p una hida. Modo pro
nichilo. qa tota. ē in foresta. excepto. i. ac pti. Tra
fuit. ii. car. Valuit. xxx. solid.

Edward Sarisberie ten. ii. hid in Alwinetune
7 Robt de eo. has tenuer. ii. alodiarii in paragio.
Tc p. ii. hid. m p nichilo qa tota sunt in foresta.
exceptis. xii. acris pti. Tra fuit. iiii. car. Valb. c. sol.

Rannulf flanbard ten de rege. i. hid in Bile.
Aluuold tenuit in paragio. Tc se defd p una hida.
m p nichilo. qa tota. ē in foresta. exceptis. iii. ac pti.
Isde Ran tenuit in ipsa uilla. i. hidā. 7 p tanto se
defd. T.R.E. Modo. ē tota in foresta. exceptis. iii.
acris pti. Tra fuit. iiii. car. He duæ træ ualb. iii. lib.

Isd Ran ten de rege. i. hid in Becheslei. Duo alodi
arii tenuer. Tc p. i. hida. m p. iii. v. Tra. ē. ii. car.
Ibi. iii. uitti hnt. i. car. 7 ii. ac pti 7 dim. Valuit. xv. sol.
Modo. iii. solid. 7 moliñ de. xxx. denar. In Rodbrige hd.

Hugo fili Osmundi ten de rege. i. hid in Bariforde.
Aluric tenuit in paragio. Tc p una hida. m p nichilo.
qa. ē in foresta. Tra fuit. iii. car. Valb. xxv. solid.

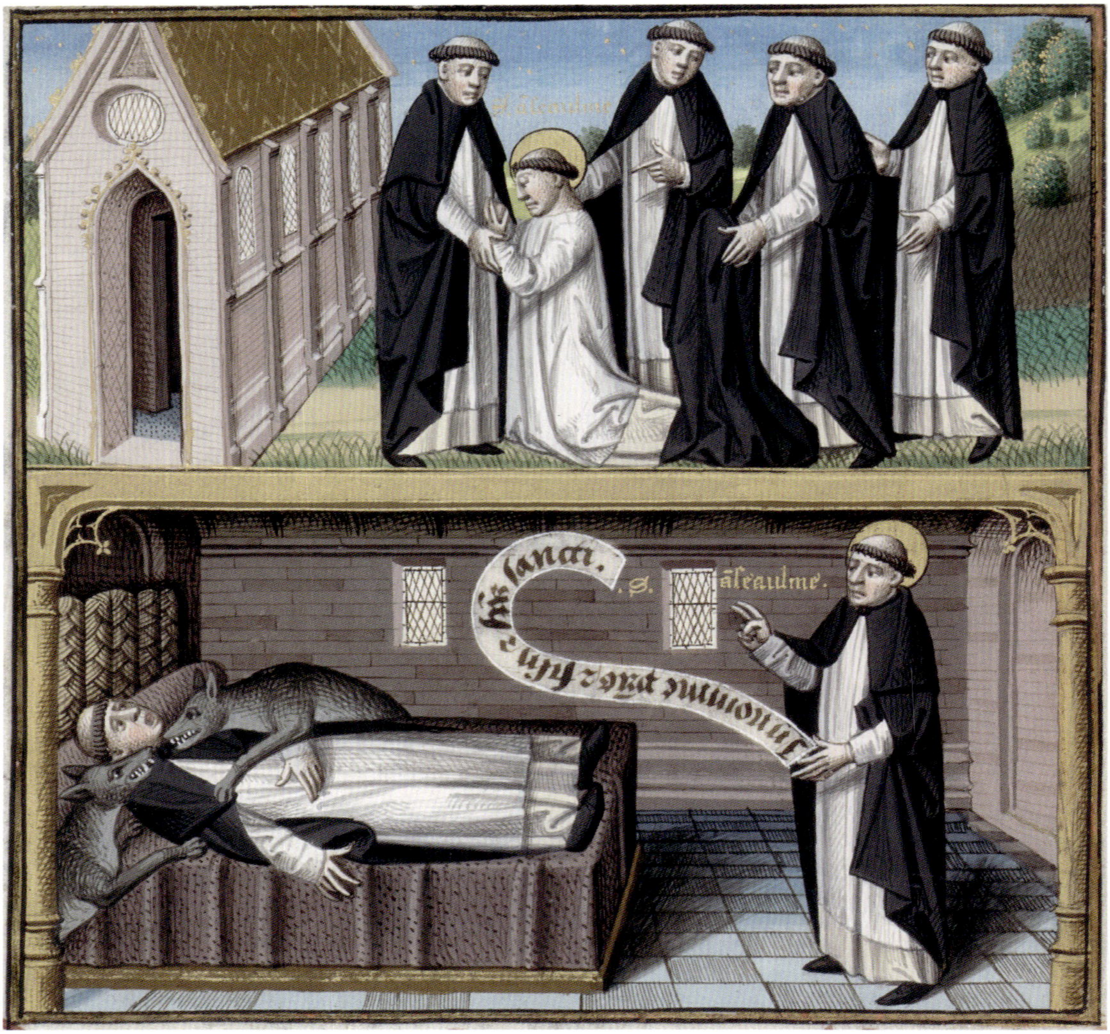

Scenes from the life of Saint Anselm of Canterbury.
Vincent of Beauvais, 'Le miroir historial', 15th century. Chantilly, Musée Condé, Ms. 722, fol. 170 v°.

Like a queen

After 1056, Eustace II began to administer his territories with the help of household officers who were not kin. But Countess Ida played an important role in the governance of the family's lands as well. She was probably the moving force behind the reconciliation between her husband and William the Conqueror. She held five manors in England directly from the king: Kingweston (Dorset), Bockhampton, Swanage and Winterbourne Monkton (Somerset) and Nutfield (Surrey). She suggested to Bishop Drogo and his successor archdeacon Hubert of Thérouanne to establish Saint-Jean au Mont as a dependency of the Norman ducal abbey of Jumièges. Acting from her landed base around Tongres and her dowry of Gennapes, she supported her son Godfrey's efforts to govern Lorraine in the early 1080's.

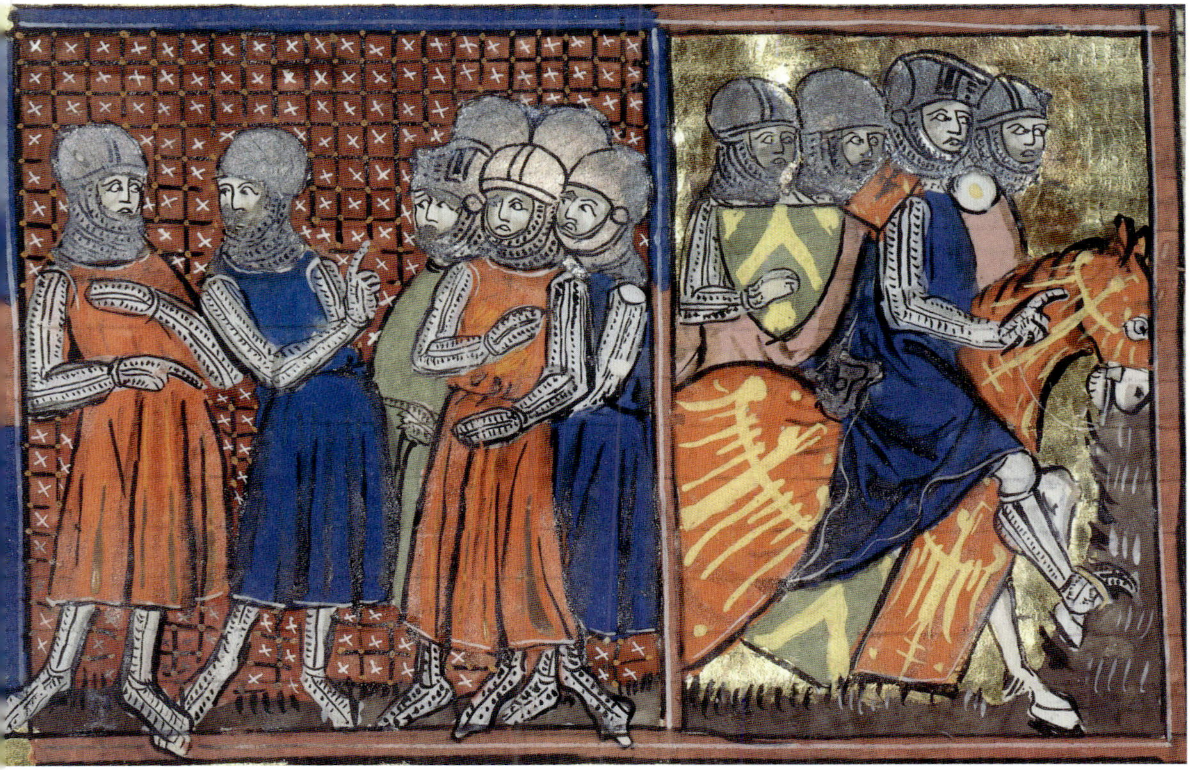

Godfrey of Bouillon reprimands his brother Baldwin.
William of Tyr, 'Historia', 14th century.
Paris, Bibliothèque Nationale de France, Mss. Français 22495, fol. 34 v°.

Ida built up a network of ecclesiastical friends. She corresponded with Saint Anselm of Canterbury until her death and she promoted, under his supervision, the Cluniac reform movement. She granted Bec land in Boulogne. The Spanish Bishop Osmond of Astorga sent her, with the permission of King Alphonso VI, some hairs of the Virgin Mary. She convinced Hugh of Cluny to send monks to populate her new foundation of Le Wast. Her ecclesiastical patronage was meant to enhance the family's prestige and strengthen their authority.

Foundations

In 1070, Eustace and Ida confirmed the college of Lens' properties and granted additional gifts. They made the grant for the remedy of their souls, but also to display their beneficent authority.
The abbey of Saint-Wulmer-au-Bois (in Samer), founded in the 7th century, was in ruins by the end of the 11th century. Eustace III and his mother Ida decided to reconstruct it. From that moment on, the counts of Boulogne were buried in the abbey church, but their graves were violated during the French Revolution.
The countess founded the Benedictine priory (later abbey) of Le Wast around 1095. She was buried there in 1113.
In 1090, Ida decided to found an abbey called La Capelle ou Capelette (in Les Attaques, near Calais). Ida was fond of the place because of its quietude. She often stayed there to join in the services held by the monks. The chronicler Lambert of Ardres writes that Ida donated the gold reliquary with twelve hairs of the Virgin Mary, given to her by king Alphonse VI of Spain, to the abbey. The abbey was totally destroyed by the English in 1346.

Construction of the Church of Our Lady at Boulogne-sur-Mer. 'Manière de la foundation et augmentation de l'église Notre-Dame de Boulogne', 15th century. Bibliothèque nationale de France, Bibliothèque de l'Arsenal, Mss. 5126, fol. 13 v°.

Ida constructed the church of Boulogne-sur-Mer in the period 1080-1110. The building was ravaged several times and finally destroyed in 1789. The beautiful crypt from Ida's time was re-discovered in 1827 during the digging of the foundations for the new church. The altar with the statue of Saint Ida (sculpted by Léon Noël) was consecrated in 1913 on the occasion of the 800th anniversary of her death.
Ida built the abbey church of Saint-Wulmer in Boulogne in around 1093, opposite of the castle of the counts of Boulogne. The building was destroyed during the French revolution.
Ida restored the Abbey of Saint-Wulmer in Samer (close to Boulogne-sur-Mer), and made many donations to the Abbey of Munsterbilzen (Limburg, Belgium), where she was educated.

Basilica of Our Lady, Boulogne-sur-Mer.

Landscape: rue des Cappes at Les Attaques, the site where the Abbey of La Capelle used to stand.

Room with the cenotaph of Godfrey of Bouillon in the crypt of the Basilica of Our Lady in Boulogne-sur-Mer.

Site of the former abbey of Saint-Wulmer-au-Bois, restored by Ida of Boulogne. Samer, Place de l'Abbaye.

Tomb of Godfrey of Bouillon.
Frank Moore Colby, Outlines of General History, New York: American Book Company, 1899, p. 265

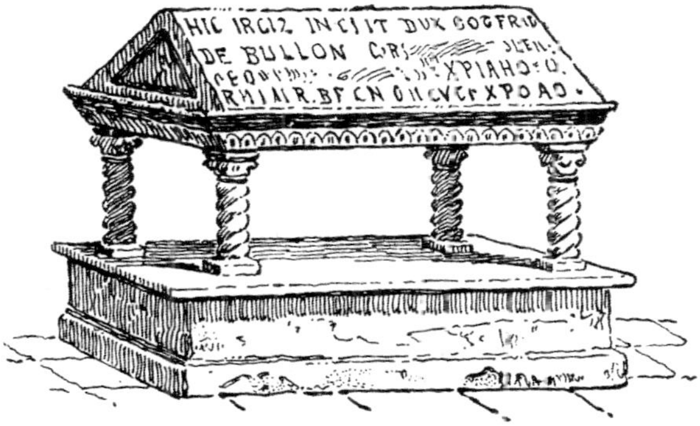

Frame containing relics of four saints, among them Saint Ida. 19th century. Malzéville, Eglise paroissiale Saint-Martin.

Ph. G. André © Région Lorraine - Inventaire general.

Reliquary containing the only surviving piece of the miraculous statue of Our Lady of the Sea. Boulogne-sur-Mer, Treasury of the Basilica.

A relic is a part of the body of a saint or an object that is closely related to the saint. The word comes from the Latin *reliquiae* meaning 'remains'. Relics are venerated as a tangible memory of the saint through which God can perform miracles. The Second Council of Nicaea in 787 decreed that every altar should contain a relic. This is still the case today.
The tales of miracles attributed to relics were recorded. These miracle tales made that relics became much sought after during the Middle Ages. By the late Middle Ages the collecting of, and dealing in, relics had reached enormous proportions. And since people often made pilgrimages to shrines of saints, relics became big business.

Relics

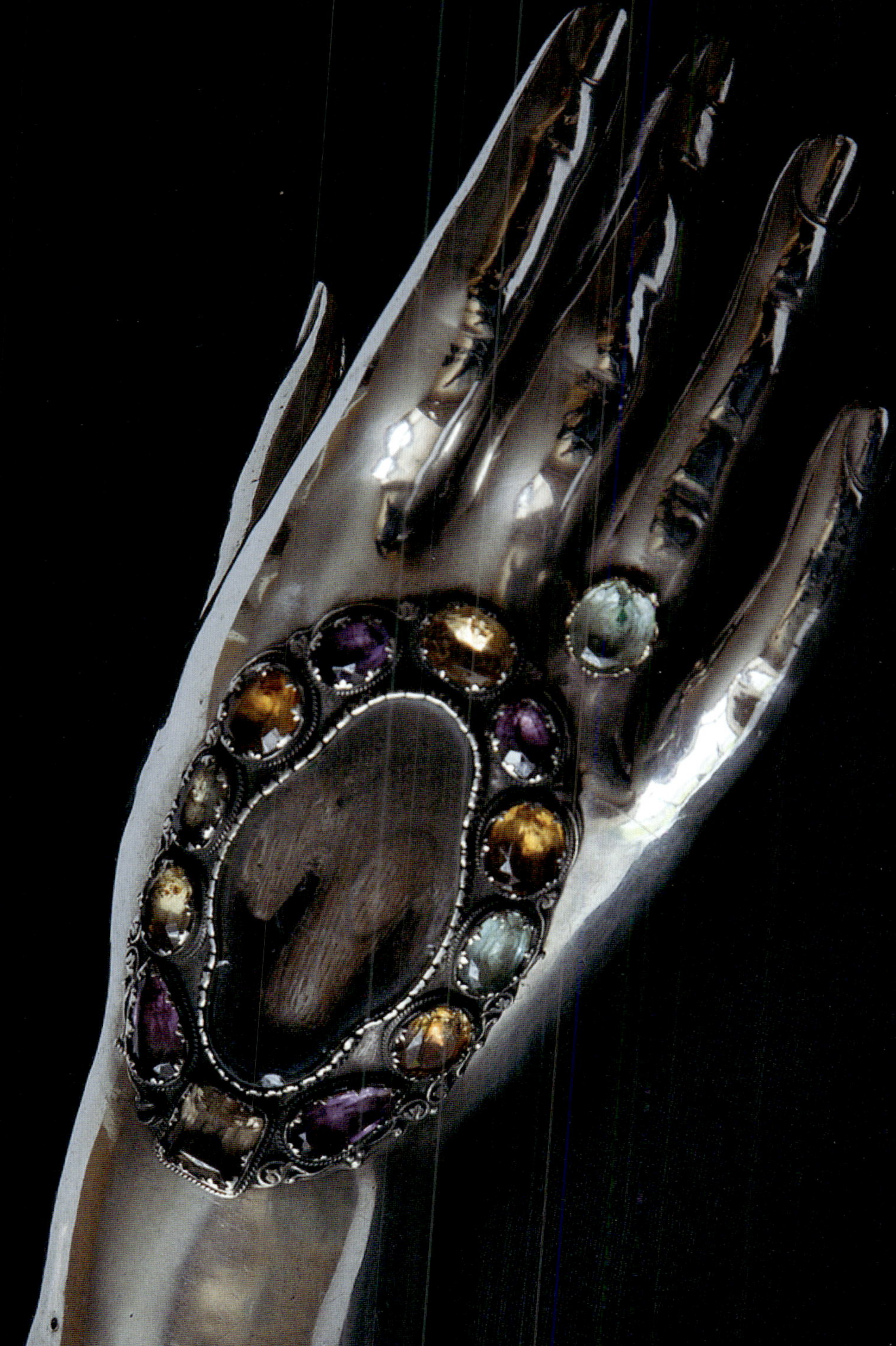

Shrine containing the relics of Saint Ida (front) in the church of the Benedictines in Bayeux.

Relics

Ida of Boulogne died on 13 April 1113 in La Capelle at the age of 73. According to her last wishes, her body was brought to the monastery of Le Wast to be buried there.

In the 17th century, the place where she was buried was in lamentable condition. Her grave was opened on 28 September 1669, and her bones were placed in a cassette, which was brought to Margaret of Lorraine, duchess of Orléans, wife of Gaston of Orléans, uncle of King Louis XIV. Margaret made two reliquaries. One of the two, made of ivory and containing most of the remains, was given to the nuns of the Holy Sacrement in the rue Cassette in Paris. The other one contained a rib of the saint and was given to the church of Le Wast.

Shrine containing the relics of Saint Ida (back) in the church of the Benedictines in Bayeux.

Portrait of Jean Marie Henriau, bishop of Boulogne from 1724 to 1738. Boulogne-sur-Mer, Basilique Notre-Dame.

An unknown lady saved the relic of Le Wast and restored it to the church after the French Revolution. The relic was examined; the reliquary was closed and sealed by the Bishop Cardinal. They were authenticated on 31 October 1883.

The relics of Paris were saved by one of the nuns who brought them to the Benedictine monastery of Bayeux, where they remain to this day. The reliquary was opened again at the instigation of Mgr. Amette, bishop of Bayeux, in 1899 and a fragment of the ulna was sent to the church of Our Lady in Boulogne-sur-Mer. According to the nuns of Bayeux, in 1923, some of the bones were sent to the Benedictine abbey of Saint-Omer and to the church of Bouillon.

Remains of the Abbey of La Capelle. Les Attaques, Ferme Pédagogique "Les Cappes".

The church of Le Wast, where Ida was buried.

Cathedral in Bayeux.

Fire at the palace of Bouillon.
'Le Chevalier au Cygne',
13th century. Paris, Bibliothèque
Nationale de France, Mss. Français
786, fol. 124.

The story of the Swan Knight is a medieval tale about a mysterious knight who arrives in a swan-drawn boat to defend a young lady. He stays with her under the only condition that she never asks his name.

The tale exists in different versions. In one version, the Swan Knight's adventures bring him to the defence of the dispossessed Duchess of Bouillon, whose land has been seized by Regnier of Saxony, whom he challenges to a duel. The Swan Knight defeats Regnier and wins the daughter of the Duchess in marriage. They have a daughter, Ida, who can see the future and knows that she is destined to be the mother of Eustace, Godfrey, and Baldwin. The Swan Knight, however, must leave Bouillon when his wife asks him to reveal his true identity.

In 1848, Richard Wagner adapted the tale into his popular opera Lohengrin, probably the work through which the Swan Knight story is best known today.

The swan in the coat of arms of Boulogne refers to the legend of the Swan Knight. Town hall of Boulogne-sur-Mer.

The Swan Knight

Lohengrin's arrival (in Brabant). Painting by August von Heckel, 1882/83. Schloss Neuschwanstein, Mural in the Salon.

Memory

Reliquary containing a rib of Saint Ida in the church of Le Wast.

In spite of all the efforts, the worship of Ida of Boulogne was never widely spread. She was not remembered as a saint, but as the mother of Godfrey of Bouillon and Baldwin I of Jerusalem. In the Old French *Cycle de la Croisade,* she is the daughter of the Swan Knight *(Le Chevalier au Cygne)*, who married the Count of Boulogne. It was especially her son Godfrey of Bouillon, a hero of the First Crusade, who appealed to the imagination. The chronicler Guibert of Nogent tells us that Ida herself told heroic stories about her son Godfrey; how as a child he was constantly saying that he would go to Jerusalem at the head of a strong army: *The glorious woman used to say, when she marvelled at the result of the journey and the success of her sons, that she had heard from the mouth of her son the duke a prediction of the outcome long before the beginning of the expedition. For he said that he wanted to go to Jerusalem not as a simple pilgrim, as others had done, but forcefully, with a large army, if he could raise one.*

Saint Ida makes her son vomit. 'Enfance Godefroi', 13th century. Bibliothèque nationale de France, Mss. Français 786, fol. 138.

Closure

Glass stained window representing Saint Ida. Baltzenheim, Eglise paroissiale Saint-Michel.

Cliché Michèle Bardout ©

Région Alsace - Inventaire general.

The count and the saint. The count was a hero, of most noble birth, a brave knight, but also an adroit player of the strategic game of his time. The saint was a woman, descending from Charlemagne, very pious, but also a lady of power and a great mother. Together they formed the heart of a glorious and famous family in an important and strategic region. To follow the traces they left makes for a fascinating journey through history.

Bouillon

The castle of Bouillon is first mentioned in 988, although its history may go back much further in time. It is situated on a rocky spur of land within a sharp bend of the Semois River. The castle was built on a strategic place to control the north-south passage between Upper and Lower Lorraine. The Dukes of the House of Ardenne owned the castle until 1096, when Godfrey of Bouillon sold it to Otbert, Prince-Bishop of Liège in order to finance the first crusade. Otbert desperately wanted to own this strategically important area and therefore plundered the abbeys and monasteries of his own diocese in order to raise the necessary funds for the purchase.

In 1676, the troops of the French king Louis XIV besieged and captured the castle. The famous military engineer Vauban improved the defences of the town and castle. He built nine tower bastions connected by curtain walls to enclose the town and added a high loop-holed wall to the caste. The castle remained a military fortress until the 19th century.

Today the castle is the oldest and best preserved construction from feudal times in Belgium. Overlooking the small town of Bouillon, it is the main tourist attraction for the region.

Boulogne-sur-Mer

The town of Boulogne, at the mouth of the river Liane, has been an important port since medieval times. It became the centre base of the counts of Boulogne. The first donjon was built by count Renaud de Dammartin at the end of the 12th century. It was abandoned for a new castle in the 13th century. The donjon became the Belfrey, still visible today and since 2005 a UNESCO world heritage site. The castle was later used as barracks and was a prison until 1974. Now it is a museum.

A relic containing the Holy Blood of Christ is preserved in the museum. According to the legend, Godfrey of Bouillon sent this relic from the Holy Land to Bouillon. His mother, Ida of Boulogne, was waiting for the relic and received it somewhere on the outskirts of the town.

On this spot, a chapel was built in the 19th century, the *Chapelle Notre-Dame du Saint-Sang*, situated along the avenue Kennedy. A bas-relief above the entrance represents Saint Ida receiving the relic.

The present day Basilica of Notre-Dame was built in the 19th century, after the former cathedral had been destroyed in the course of the French Revolution. While constructing the basilica, the remains of the 11th century crypt were discovered, restored and preserved. They are part of the first stone church of Boulogne-sur-Mer, built by countess Ida of Boulogne. In one of the rooms, a cenotaph in honour of Godfrey of Bouillon was erected.

Bayeux

The town of Bayeux is situated only a few kilometres from Omaha Beach, Juno Beach and Gold Beach. Being the first town liberated at the end of the Second World War, it is very much associated with the invasion of Normandy by the allied forces on 6 June 1944. But Bayeux is also and foremost a town with a rich medieval history, celebrated each summer in the *Fêtes médievales*. Strolling along the river Aure or walking past the timber frame houses, one can experience the medieval spirit of the town.
The impressive cathedral of Notre-Dame was built in the 11th century, started by Hugo, bishop of Bayeux, and finished by his successor Odo. The church was consecrated on 14 July 1077 in the presence of William the Conqueror, duke of Normandy and king of England, also Odo's half-brother. On this occasion, the splendid Bayeux Tapestry was displayed for the first time. This seventy meters long embroidery depicts the events leading up to the Norman Conquest of England, culminating in the Battle of Hastings. It has been listed as a *Memory of the World* by UNESCO since 2007. It is now displayed in the *Musée de la Tapisserie de Bayeux*.

For a long time, it was assumed that the tapestry was commissioned by Odo of Bayeux, but recent research names Eustace, count of Boulogne, as the patron of the embroidery. The count and countess of Boulogne, Eustace and Ida, almost certainly were present at the inauguration of the cathedral and the first showing of the tapestry.
Less known is the abbey of the Benedictines in the Rue Saint Loup. The abbey was founded in Bayeux in the 17th century and was located in the ceramics district. The nuns were dispersed with the French Revolution and the buildings were confiscated. But soon the sisters resumed community life in the former house of the Franciscans, where they rebuilt their monastery. The lovely 19th century church houses the beautiful shrine containing the relics of Saint Ida.

CAP
2012 !

Pevensey, Hastings and Battle

On 28 September 1066, William the Conqueror and his fleet landed unopposed at Pevensey. The local stronghold had been abandoned after Harold Godwinson had rushed his army northward to fight the invading Harald Hardrada. Shortly after the Norman Conquest, Pevensey was granted to Robert, count of Mortain, half-brother of William the Conqueror. He transformed the fort into a castle. It is now a Scheduled Monument in the care of English Heritage and is open to visitors.

The Battle of Hastings between the armies of William the Conqueror and Harold Godwinson took place on 14 October 1066 at Senlac Hill, roughly ten kilometres from Hastings. Battle Abbey marks the site where the Battle was fought. In 1070, Pope Alexander II ordered the Normans to do penance for killing so many people during their conquest of England. So William the Conqueror vowed to build an abbey where the Battle of Hastings had taken place, with the high altar of its church on the supposed spot where King Harold was killed. It was finished in about 1094 and consecrated during the reign of the Conqueror's son William Rufus. The abbey was remodelled in the late 13th century but virtually destroyed during the Dissolution of the Monasteries under King Henry VIII.

A plaque on the ground now marks the spot where Harold fell, and a monument to Harold erected by the people of Normandy in 1903 stands nearby. The Grade I listed site is now

operated by English Heritage as *1066 Battle of Hastings, Abbey and Battlefield*, which includes the abbey buildings and ruins, a visitor centre with a film and exhibition on the battle, audio tours of the battlefield site, and the monks' gatehouse with recovered artefacts. The site is also the location of annual re-enactments of the battle of Hastings.

Bibliography

J. C. Andressohn, *The Ancestry and Life of Godfrey of Bouillon*, Bloomington, 1947.

F. Barlow, *Edward the Confessor*, Oxford, 1997.

A. Bridgeford, 'Was Count Eustace II of Boulogne the patron of the Bayeux Tapestry?', in: *Journal of Medieval History*, 25/3 (1999), pp. 155-185.

A. Bridgeford, 'Whose Tapestry is it Anyway?', in: *History Today*, 54 (2004).

A. Bridgeford, *1066: The Hidden History in the Bayeux Tapestry*, New York, 2005.

S. A. Brown, 'The Bayeux tapestry: why Eustace, Odo, and William?', in: *Anglo-Norman Studies*, XII (1989), pp. 7-28.

R. D'amat, 'Eustache, comte de Boulogne', in: *Dictionnaire de Biographie Française*, 13, col. 271-272.

J. P. Dickès, *Sainte Ide de Boulogne*, Paris, 2004.

G. Duby, *The knight, the lady and the priest*, Chicago, 1983 [pp. 135-138: Ida of Boulogne].

F. Ducatel, *Vie de Sainte Ide de Lorraine, comtesse de Boulogne*, Boulogne, 1900.

B. De Gaiffier, 'Sainte Ide de Boulogne et l'Espagne', in: *Analecta Bollandiana*, 86 (1968), 67-82.

E. Dunlop, *Queen Margaret of Scotland*, Edinburgh, 2005.

J. A. Green, *The Aristocracy of Norman England*, Cambridge, 1997.

Guibert de Nogent, Dei Gesta per Francos, ed. R.B.C. HUYGENS, *Corpus Christianorum, Continuatio Mediaevalis* 127A, Turnhout, 1996.

Guy d'Amiens, *Carmen de Hastingae Proelio*, ed. and trans. F. BARLOW, Oxford, 1999.

W. A. Hammond, 'A Treatise on insanity in its medical relations', in: *British Juournal of Psychiatry*, 29 (January 1884), pp. 579-585.

F. Holböck, *Married Saints and Blesseds through the centuries*, San Francisco, 2002. [Ida of Boulogne: 146-147; Margaret of Scotland: 144-146]

E. Van Houts, 'Edward and Normandy', in R. Mortimer ed., *Edward the Confessor: The Man and the Legend*, Woodbridge, 2009.

N. Huyghebaert, 'La mère de Godefroid de Bouillon, la comtesse Ide de Boulogne', in: *Publications de la section historique de l'institut Grand-Ducal de Luxembourg*, 95 (1981), pp. 43-63.

K. S. B. Keats-Rohan, *Domesday People. A Prosopography of Persons Occurring in English documents 1066-1166. I. Domesday Book*, Woodbridge, 1999 [pp. 196-197: Eustachius Comes].

Lambert of Ardres, *The History of the Counts of Guines and Lords of Ardres*, ed. and trans. L. SHOPKOW, Philadelphia, 2000.

S. Morillo, *The Battle of Hastings: Sources and Interpretation*, Woodbridge, 1996.

A. V. Murray, *The crusader kingdom of Jerusalem: a dynastic history 1099-1125*, Oxford, 2000.

R. Nip, 'Godelieve of Gistel and Ida of Boulogne', in: A.B. MULDER-BAKKER (ed.), *Sanctity and Motherhood: Essays on Holy Mothers in the Middle Ages*, New York – London, 1995.

R. Nip, 'The Political Relations between England and Flanders (1066-1128)', in: *Anglo-Norman Studies*, 21 (1999), pp. 145-167.

J. Robinson Planche, *The Conqueror and his companions*, London, 1874. [Eustace: pp. 148-160]

E. Rigaux, *Recherches sur les Premiers Comtes de Boulogne*, Boulogne, 1896.

H. J. Tanner, 'The Expansion of the Power and Influence of the Counts of Boulogne under Eustace II', in: *Anglo-Norman Studies*, 14 (1991) pp. 251-286.

H. J. Tanner, *Families, friends, and allies: Boulogne and politics in northern France and England, c. 879-1160*, Leiden 2004.

H. J. Tanner, 'Eustace (II), count of Boulogne (d. c.1087)', in: *Oxford Dictionary of National Biography*, Oxford University Press, 2004.

C. Tyerman, *God's War: A New History of the Crusades*, Cambridge, 2006.

S. N. Vaughn, 'St. Anselm and Women', in: *Haskins Society Journal*, 2 (1990), pp. 83-94.

C. Warren Hollister, 'The Greater Domesday Tenants-in-Chief', in: J.C. HOLT (ed.), *Domesday Studies*, Woodbridge, 1987.

William of Poitiers, *Gesta Guillelmi*, ed. and trans. R. H. C. DAVIS and M. CHIBNALL, Oxford, 1998.

'Ide de Boulogne', in: *Dictionnaire d'Histoire et de Géographie Ecclésiastique*, 25 (1995), col. 644-645.

Author
Horst van Cuyck

Research
in collaboration with dr. Véronique Lambert

Photography
Horst van Cuyck, with the assistance of Alan Ross

Final Editing
Michael Meert

Layout
Group Van Damme
www.groupvandamme.eu

Print
PurePrint
www.pureprint.be

Published by
Stichting Kunstboek bvba
Legeweg 165
B-8020 Oostkamp
Belgium
Tel. +32 50 46 19 10
Fax +32 50 46 19 18
info@stichtingkunstboek.com
www.stichtingkunstboek.com

ISBN 978-90-5856-445-0
D/2013/6407/6
NUR 681